365 DAYS

1ST EDITION

UTKARSH AAYUSH

Made with ♥ on the Notion Press Platform
www.notionpress.com

Contents

Preface

05:19 Hey guys! This is Utkarsh . An ordinary kid with millions of dreams and I'm pretty much sure that only few gonna complete with time and efforts. So today I'm gonna start blogging means u get my blog and u can read them or don't read them and do whatever with it today. I don't really care about it . But the thing that I'm caring about is I'm going to start a new thing today and that's important for me. I'm starting this thing with a lot of happiness. I'm happy cause from now u can check what's going in my life yeah it's cool for people who want to check for what's I'm actually doing in my life without letting a clue that they know about me or as simple u can call them as stalker. So from now I let all of my audience to check what's going in my life. I'm gonna share some experience and what I think about things in my life. Hope you'll enjoy it cause I'm a crazy person and my life is more crazy than me . I'm going to start a novel sort of things and I'm going to name it "365 days" every single day is like 1 chapter and every chapter will come with a new beginning.

1

365 DAYS : DAY 1

05:05 Hello! I'm back again with a smile. I know you can't see it cause it's a blog so just feel it. Recently I faced a problem with my emotions. I don't know about you guys who is currently sitting on sofa and chair or lying in bed and reading this .Have you felt the same or not but let me tell you all about it. So there was one of my friends to whom I told that I'm heading to start a new story like thing in my site ,you wanna hear it . The answer was 'no'. I was kind of hurt. You know we use to call us as best friends and I thought best friends always support each other but I failed at that moment. You know when everyone is supporting you in your life to move forward only one 'no' can shatter all your confidence about heading a new start. I felt like I should stop but then I thought of friends who supported me and there was one friend who was like angel to me. I recommended the same thing to her and the answer was "yes, I can visit what you up to". That's the one cause of which I got my confidence back and I'm here still writing. You know sometimes a yes and a no is very much powerful to people whom you are telling this too. So, be always aware of what's your yes or no is going to impact the person standing in front of you.

2

365DAYS :DAY2

08:28 Hello! It's awesome to see you buddies again . Sorry today I'm late in posting my blog , got a headache which didn't let me write. It's a 3 hours' delay cause of my headache. So last day was one of the greatest day of my life . The support everyone gave me to my first story was amazing . The whole day I was thinking of the next topic what to write for my next day . Then after I saw a comment . Thise comment tried to tell me that not in every part of life everyone is with you rather there is only one person who can stand with you and that person is you yourself. I appreciate it but I disagree many people who told me this before that you have to walk on the path alone . Humans are species which are totally interdependent on each other ,without anyone else we can't do anything. There are always people around us who helps us a lot in our journey of life . For a child ,his parents are the supporter .When he grows up ,he gets friends to support him and after marriage he gets a life partner that will stay with him for the rest of the life. If you all think that if someone doesn't have any of them then my point is null but no. There is always one who is supporting all the time without letting us know, he gives us hope and faith and is a source of immortal superpower and we name him as GOD . So if you think that no one is supporting you ,think twice cause there are always people who are supporting you . Don't say that you are alone, you were never and never going to be.

3

365DAYS:DAY3

06:50 Good morning fellow readers. You know sometimes when I'm hanging in my balcony, my eyes caught an old man walking through streets and there's a specific reason why my eyes gave so much attention to him. From so many years I have seen him walking and the fact is he can't barely walk, he can only move his feet few centimetres. So it takes him almost an hour to take a round trip of the distance which I used to cover in 10 mins . The fact is he can't walk like others but he is not giving up rather he is still walking on streets and challenging his life. I met an another person on social media. The person has a disease called celiac. In this ,we can't eat the food items which includes wheat in it. As an Indian wheat plays an important role in our life. So I thought is there any other stuff rather and I get my answer there r many. So the person can't eat wheat in life. If that situation came to me I will became sad for sure , but that person is so happy in her life. From these two persons I got a thing that there are people around us who use to challenge life rather than giving up. Then why some of us commit suicide after losing something. These two persons have lost many wonderful moments of their life and still stay happy. We have to take inspiration from them. And you know ,there are not only these two persons in the world but there are many people in this world who can become our inspiration. Just check out across your life and I'm sure you'll get one. Take the inspiration from them and keep moving in life rather than to think of death.

4

365DAYS : DAY4

08:39 Hey yo! With a new morning I'm here to take your time with my story. So nowadays everyone around me is saying the world is suffering due to a virus called Covid-19 . Well in my opinion it's not true only humans are suffering cause of it. The world is healing from this virus. We humans made this world so dirty . I guess this is the way of God to take virus as a broom and removing all the dust. Everyone is watching negative impact like people are dying everyday cause of this but on the other hand, only few watch the positive impact. It's like the environment need a break from humans and they got it. Now you can see the sky is clear, the rivers which use to be always full of dirt particles is now cleaning. No more sound noise of horns, machines and industry. Due to this, we actually find out lost humanity . Like if this was a normal day everyone will move on street without caring of the next person walking besides him , but due to this situation now everyone is trying to help each other. Many are working with NGOs to give food and all necessary supplement to needy ones. Doctors and police officers are doing their best to secure an individual life. Cause of this ,many awesome things happens. We get our humanity of helping others back and the nature is healing . The Economy is decreasing. So I guess after all this we need to do a fresh start. It's like a game, we've reached too far and lost. Now, It's the time to try again and restart the game.

5

365DAYS : DAY5

10:01 Good morning! Sorry it's too late to say good morning. I'm late today as I was thinking of any new idea to write but got nothing. Then after I told this all to my mom that I'm having no ideas to write today, should I skip today? She told ,"there are your friends and family who are eagerly waiting for your story to read , so don't do it for yourself, but write for them cause they are waiting". She told me to go and take a shower so your mind will refresh and it really worked . So I'm writing this cause of my mother and going to write on GIRLS . Girl word is quite common to all but only few people get it's importance . As I've my mother and many family members who supports me a lot on my stories and I have some awesome friends who always support me in any situation. They never show that they are helping you but they do in every part of your life. They are like second god to us . They always let us move to the right direction. No matter though how much sadness they are going through, they always want to see you happy . My mom , family members and friends ....I've an amazing close bond to each one of them and they never let me down in any part of my life. They always prove that their presence is important for my success. I'll write about boys day after tomorrow.

6

365DAYS : DAY 6

06:21 Hey yo! morning to all. It's like a week is going to complete in this story. From the past 7 days what an enormous support I'm getting on my stories . I'm very thankful that I've got such supportive family and friends . With every single comment, I feel energetic to create the next story. Thank you all for supporting me on this journey of life . You know whenever you guys comment on my stories I'm boosted to write the next one . Keep supporting keep loving . From the start my life is like whenever I start a new thing the support rate is very high in that. This all is happening cause I'm having only pure souls around me . A BIG THANK YOU TO ALL MY VIEWERS YOUR SUPPORT GIVE ME STRENGTH. Today is a special day for me as it comes once a year . Today is my father's b'day and he is my ideal in life . LOVE YOU DAD!

7

365 DAYS : DAY 7&8

09:41 Hey! Good morning . Again I'm here with a new blog. Yesterday it was my dad's b'day and today is of mom's. Last day we celebrated a lot and now I'm waiting for today's fun. Dad is one of the person in my life whom I respect a lot. And I'm scared a lot of him if I done anything wrong. Dad always supports us and gets angry when we did a small mistake. Butcause of this toughness we become strong enough to face this world. So today's topic is boys . Let me tell you some important points of boys . They don't share everything with everyone but when they do, you're damn special. They are easy to talk about your problems, they judge less and listen more. They don't share their pain easily which even destroyes them sometimes. They do a lot and never get enough in return. They pretend that they don't care but the truth is that they show it in their actions rather than words. They have feelings and cry as well, but they prefer not to show it and supress their emotions unless you're the only one . I hope you'll like this one.

8

365 DAYS : DAY 9

08:43 Morning all! Time is a precious part of life. It plays very important role in our life. Some people didn't gets the importance of time and when they realise it everything is gone . For our all round development we must judge the time in order to achieve our aim and object. Those who utilise the right timing they never fail and their life becomes prosperous and always remains happy. Time is one of the best medicine it heals the pains of our souls. Hard work and proper timing help us to achieve our goal. We should therefore do not waste time and remain continuing our works of life which will help us to attain our all round development. Therefore don't let your precious time to leave you so that you will feel sorry in future about it.

9

365 DAYS : DAY 10

11:50 Hey yo! Utkarsh here . Nowadays everyone is in tension of when will this pandemic going to end?But there are people who are enjoying it ,like those who don't have jobs they are enjoying by watching the boss of the company where he has been rejected in the interview. They are like yo boss .Now they can feel my pain of staying at home . And children, who are in school are really confused ....they always wished to get 6 months holidays twice a year and now they are getting it then they are missing school so much. The child brain is so confusing ....they don't want to go to school ,....now they've got a chance then they want to go to school....... seriously so confusing. Most people have changed their routine of eating, sleeping and repeating. Some people are in a hope that when the lockdown will open, I'll show the world that I've become stronger. But the fact is they have become fatty more than stronger. Those people who likes to work all day are now feeling bored. Due to this , the cellphone companies are getting massive profit . Now, no one cares about using phone only for two hours ,they are like I switched off my phone cause I'm bored after 5 minutes but again they are using phones cause they are bored. Well, most people are becoming lazy nowadays but those who are still working on their dream in this hard time is the one who is going to rise and shine after this pandemic. So life is so hard but you've to find a way to keep working and the one who stops in this hard life will be thrown behind. So, don't stop in this race...... keep running keep working. Happy pandemic to all.

365 Days : End Of First Edition

07:32 Hi guys, so i hope you all love reading all of my stories. There is a lot going to come in the 2nd edition. But for now I am ending the first edition here. Keep supporting and i will keep on publisihing new stories, new chapter with some new days. see ya from utkarsh.

Printed by Libri Plureos GmbH in Hamburg, Germany